Edwin William Streeter

The Koh-i-Nur Diamond

Its romance and history; with special notes by Her Majesty the Queen.

Also the curious history of the celebrated Pitt diamond, with special notes

by the ex-Empress Eugenie

Edwin William Streeter

The Koh-i-Nur Diamond
*Its romance and history; with special notes by Her Majesty the Queen. Also the
curious history of the celebrated Pitt diamond, with special notes by the ex-Empress
Eugenie*

ISBN/EAN: 9783337321482

Printed in Europe, USA, Canada, Australia, Japan

Cover: Foto ©ninafisch / pixelio.de

More available books at **www.hansebooks.com**

THE

KOH-I-NÛR

DIAMOND.

Its Romance and History.

With SPECIAL NOTES by
HER MAJESTY THE QUEEN.

Also the Curious History of the Celebrated
PITT DIAMOND,
With SPECIAL NOTES by
THE EX-EMPRESS EUGENIE.

•:•

REPRINTED FROM "GREAT DIAMONDS OF THE
WORLD," BY EDWIN W. STREETER, F.R.G.S.,
&c., &c.

•:•

LONDON : GEORGE BELL & SONS,
YORK ST., COVENT GARDEN, 1895.

HOWLETT AND SON, PRINTERS, 10, FRITH-ST., LONDON, W.

" THe history of the Koh-i-Noor Diamond is one long romance, and is well authenticated at every step. History never lost sight of its fate from the days when Ala-ud-deen took it from the Rajahs of Malwa, five centuries and a half ago, and tradition carries back its existence in the memory of India to the half mystic hero, Bikramajèet,—better known as Vikramaditya, the expeller of the Scythians from India—Rajah of Usjein and Malwa, 57 B.C. A wilder legend recognises it as a Diamond worn by Carna, Rajah of Anga. The stone is said to have been found in the bed of the Godavery river, near Masulipatam, 5000 years ago.

Baber states that it came into the Delhi Treasury, A.D. 1304."

PROFESSOR MASKELYNE.

XI.

THE KOH-I-NÛR:

THE GREAT DIAMOND OF HISTORY AND ROMANCE.

It will interest the reader to know that Her Majesty the Queen graciously read this chapter in manuscript, without requesting any correction or alteration in the leading points of our history. No one, we believe, has studied more carefully the records of India than the Queen, and on this account we felt that her Majesty would be pleased to recognise our effort to tell the complete story of the Koh-i-Nûr so far as to permit us to submit the MS. for her approval. This does not, of course, pledge Her Majesty to an endorsement of the facts, but it is, to some extent, an added guarantee of the correctness of our researches, and it gives a lustre to our work, for which we are loyally grateful.

The Koh-i-Nûr is pre-eminently the "Great Diamond of history and romance." Its stirring adventures, when divorced from all connection with Tavernier's " Great

Mogul," become intelligible enough. The first distinct and authentic reference to the " Koh-i-Nûr " occurs in the subjoined passage from the *Memoirs of Sultan Baba*, the author of which was a direct descendant of Tamerlane, and founder of the so-called Mogul Empire in Hindostan. Under the date of May 4, 1526, the Sultan writes :

" Bikermâjit, a Hindoo, who was Rajah of Gwalior, had governed that country for upwards of a hundred years. In the battle* in which Ibrahim was defeated, Bikermâjit was sent to hell.† Bikermâjit's family and the heads of his clan were at

---

* Baber refers to the great Battle of Pariput, April 21, 1526, in which the emperor Ibrahim, of the Afghan Lodi dynasty was overthrown, and which led to the establishment of the Tabar or "Mogul" dynasty on the throne of Delhi.

† "The charitable mode in which a good Mussulman signifies the death of an infidel."

—Leyden and Eskine.

this moment in Agra. When Hûmaiûn*
arrived, Bikermâjit's people attempted to
escape, but were taken by the parties which
Hûmaiûn had placed upon the watch, and
put in custody. Hûmaiûn did not permit
them to be plundered. Of their own free
will they presented to Hûmaiûn a 'peshkesh' (tribute or present), consisting of a
quantity of jewels and precious stones.
Among these was one famous diamond,
which had been acquired by Sultan Ala-
ed-din. It is so valuable that a judge of
diamonds valued it at half of the daily
expense of the whole world. It is about
eight mishkels. On my arrival, Hûmaiûn
presented it to me as a peshkesh, and
I gave it back to him as a present."
That the diamond here referred to is

---

* Hûmaiûn was the favourite son and successor
of Baber, as emperor of Hindostan.

the "Koh-i-Nûr," there can be no reasonable doubt; nor indeed has the fact ever been seriously called into question. It will be noticed that, although he speaks of it as already "famous," Baber gives it no particular name, and it did not take its present designation till it passed into the hands of Nadir Shah. The illustrious historian mentions, however, that it "had been acquired by Sultan Ala-ed-din," which enables us to trace its existence some two hundred years further back. The Ala-ed-din here spoken of belonged to the Khilji dynasty, which succeeded that of the Ghûri, and which ruled over a large portion of Hindostan for 33 years, from A.D. 1288 to 1321, when they were replaced by the Toghlaks. Ala-ed-din Khilji had obtained possession of the "famous diamond" in the year 1304, when he defeated the Rajah of Malwa, in whose family it had been as an heirloom from time out of mind. One tradition carries it back to the somewhat legendary Vikramâditya, an ancestor of the Rajah of Malwa here spoken of, and of Baber's Bikermâjit, Rajah of Gwalior. This Vikramâditya flourished in 57 B.C., and is said to have driven the Saca (by which are no doubt meant the Scythians) out of India. But no value can attach to the tradition, which is evidently a sort of afterthought, suggested by the similarity, or rather identity, of the two names Bikermâjit and Vikramâditya. At the same time the association is significant, as it serves to show that the gem was at all times regarded as the property of the Rajahs of Malwa, who are sometimes spoken of as Rajahs of Ujein and Gwalior; for all these places were formerly included

13

in the territory of Malwa, which has since
been subdivided among the States of
Bhopal, Indore, and Gwalior—the dominions of Scindia. We now understand how
it happened that the diamond, after being
acquired by the Sultan Ala-ed-dîn in 1304,
is found in the possession of Bikermâjit,
Rajah of Gwalior in 1526. It had evidently
been restored to Bikermâjit's family by
the Khilji ruler after peace had been
established between the two states.

A still more obscure and extravagant
tradition identifies this stone with one
discovered first some 5,000 years ago, in
the bed of the Lower Godavery River,
near Masulipatam, and afterwards worn as
a sacred talisman by Carna, Rajah of Anga,
who figures in the legendary wars of the
Mahâbhârata. That such a stone should
have been found in such a place is likely

enough, as it may well have been washed down to the delta of the Godavery, which flows through one of the richest diaman-tiferous regions in the world. But its identification with the stone under consideration rests on no solid foundation, nor will it readily be believed that a gem, which remained unnamed till the eighteenth century, could be unerringly traced back to pre-historic times.

Its subsequent history from the time when it fell into the hands of Baber to the present day is inseparab'y associated with many of the most stirring and romantic events of modern days. But, to quote Maskelyne, though "one long romance from then till now, it is well authenticated at every step, as history seems never to have lost sight of this stone of fate from the days when Ala-ed-din took it from the

Rajah of Malwa, five centuries and a half ago, to the day when it became a crown jewel of England.

Bernier tells us that on the death of Shah Jehan, Aurung-zeb "set out immediately for Agra, where Begum Sahel received him with distinguished honour. On arriving at the women's apartments, the princess presented him with a large golden basin full of precious stones, her own jewels and those which belonged to Shah Jehan." The princess here referred to was Jihanara, the too well-beloved daughter of Shah Jehan, who remained with him to the last, and who had used her influence to prevent him from destroying his jewels rather than surrender them to Aurung-zeb, as mentioned in our account of the " Great Mogul." It is uncertain whether Baber's diamond was one of those contained in the golden basin, or whether it had already been given to Aurung-zeb during his father's lifetime. The former supposition seems to be the most probable ; for amongst Aurung-zeb's treasures exhibited to Tavernier, November 3, 1665, there was only one diamond of great size—the " Mogul "— and Shah Jehan, already afflicted with a fatal disease, died in the following February. But the point is of little consequence, as in any case the stone remained in the possession of the Mogul dynasty until Nadir Shah's invasion of India, during the reign of Mohammed Shah, in 1739.

In our account of the " Orloff," reference has already been made to Whittaker's statement that Aurung-zeb made use of the " Koh-i-Nûr " as one of the eyes of the peacock, adorning his

17

" Peacock Throne," and that Nadir carried off and broke up this throne, thus gaining possession of the famous gem. But according to another and apparently more trustworthy account, when he seized on the Delhi treasury this stone, which he was bent on securing, was found to be missing, and for a long time all his efforts to obtain it were baffled. At last a woman from Mohammed's harem betrayed the secret, informing Nadir that the emperor wore it concealed in his turban, which he never on any occasion laid aside.

Nadir had now recourse to a very clever trick, in order to secure the coveted prize. Having already seized on the bulk of the Delhi treasures, and concluded a treaty with the ill-fated Mogul emperor, he had no further pretext for quarrelling, and could not therefore resort to violence in order to effect his purpose. But he skilfully availed himself of a time-honoured Oriental custom, seldom omitted by princes of equal rank, on State occasions. At the grand ceremony a few days afterwards held in Delhi, for the purpose of re-instating Mohammed on the throne of his Tartar ancestors, Nadir suddenly took the opportunity of asking him to exchange turbans, in token of reconciliation, and in order to cement the eternal friendship that they had just sworn for each other. Taken completely aback by this sudden move, and lacking the leisure even for reflection, Mohammed found himself checkmated by his wily rival, and was fain, with as much grace as possible, to accept the insidious request. Indeed the Persian conqueror left him no option, for he quickly removed his own national sheepskin head-dress, glittering with costly gems, and replaced it with the emperor's turban. Maintaining the proverbial self-command of Oriental potentates Mohammed betrayed his surprise and chagrin by no outward sign, and so indifferent did he seem to the exchange, that for a moment Nadir began to fear he had been misled. Anxious to be relieved of his doubts, he hastily dismissed the durbar with renewed assurances of friendship and devotion. Withdrawing to his tent he unfolded the turban, to discover, with selfish rapture, the long coveted stone. He hailed the sparkling gem with the exclamation, "Koh i-Nûr!" signifying in English, "Mountain of Light."

At Nadir's death most of his treasures were dispersed, but the "Koh-i-Nûr," henceforth known by this title, passed together with many other jewels into the hands of his feeble son, and temporary successor, Shah Rokh. On him it brought nothing but misfortune ; yet he clung to it with amazing tenacity, refusing to part with it under pressure of the most atrocious tortures, including even loss of sight. After his overthrow, he had been permitted to reside at Meshd, as governor of that city and district. Hither he brought the " Kohi-Nûr," together with many other gems of great value, which formed part of the plunder carried off by his father from India. Aga Mohammed, who had an insatiable appetite for such things, determined to get possession of them ; and in order the more easily to effect his purpose, he advanced with a large force towards Meshd, under the pretext of visiting the sacred shrine of the Imâm Riza, which is annually resorted to by many thousands

of Shiah pilgrims. He thus succeeded in
quietly occupying the city. After per-
forming his devotions at the tomb of the
saint, suddenly throwing off all disguise, he
ordered the blind prince to deliver up his
concealed treasures. As the infatuated
Shah Rokh still protested that he had
already parted with them, he was ordered
to be put to fresh torture, which had the
effect of bringing to light several costly
gems. But as neither the " Koh-i-Nûr "
nor the immense ruby known to have been
in the crown of Aurung-zeb were amongst
them, Aga Mohammed devised a truly
diabolical expedient to get hold of them.
He ordered his victim's head to be closely
shaved and encircled with a diadem of
paste, and boiling oil to be poured into the
receptacle thus formed. But even the
frightful agony of this torture could only

induce the victim to surrender the ruby,
He still retained his hold of the great
diamond. The miserable monarch never
recovered from these injuries. Before
his death, Ahmed Shah, founder of the
Durani Afghan Empire, came to his
assistance in 1751, concluded an alliance
with him, and received in return the fatal
gem, whose brilliancy could no longer re-
joice the lack-lustre eyes of Shah Rokh.*

Possession of the unlucky gem proved
no less disastrous to the Durani dynasty
than it had to the Mogul emperors, and

---

* Early in 1751, Ahmed was recalled to Meshd
by the revolt of Mir Allum Khan (Aga Mohammed),
Chief of Kauin, who had seized on the treasure
at Meshd, and blinded and dethroned Shah Rokh
Mûrza. Ahmed restored Shah Rokh and soon
after took Kauin, and put Mir Allum to death.
Elphinstone's *Kabul*, p. 579. But according to
other accounts Shah Rokh had already been
blinded before the events here related.

to Nadir's family. At his death Ahmed Shah bequeathed it to his son and heir, Taimûr Shah, who removed the seat of government from Kandahar to Kabul, and who died in 1793. From Taimûr it descended, with the crown, to his eldest son, Shah Zamân, who was deposed and deprived of his sight by his next brother, Shah Shuja-ul-Mûlk.* The usurper thus became possessed of the "Koh-i-Nûr," which he retained almost to his death; but which, nevertheless, involved him in an uninterrupted series of calamities and sufferings. After having remained for many years concealed in the wall of a stronghold, where Shah Zamân had been confined, the diamond was brought to

---

* "The messengers met Ramûn on his way to Kabul, and performed their orders by piercing his eyes with a lancet."—Elphinstone, op, cit. p. 579.

light by the merest accident. Shah Zamân had, as he supposed, securely embedded it in the plaster of his prison wall. But in course of time a portion of plaster crumbled away, leaving one of the sharp angles of the crystal exposed, or slightly protruding on the surface. Against this one of the officials happening to scratch his hand, his attention was attracted to the spot. his eye fell on the sparkling facet, and the " Koh-i-Nûr " was once more rescued from its hiding place. At all state ceremonials Shah Shuja now wore it on his breast, where it glittered when Elphinstone was sent by the Indian Government as Envoy to Peshawur during that Prince's troubled reign.

In his turn dethroned, deprived of his sight, and driven into exile by Shah Mahmûd, third son of Taimûr, Shah Shuja had contrived, amidst all his disasters, to retain possession of the great diamond, with which he now withdrew to the court of the famous Runjìt-Singh, the "Lion of the Punjaub," accompanied by his brother, Shah Zamân, whom, as stated, he had himself already rendered sightless, according to the brutal fashion of the Durani court.

Runjìt at first received the two ill-starred brothers with open arms, and even declared war on their behalf against Shah Mahmûd, from whom he took the territory of Kashmir, which at that time formed part of the Afghan dominions. He, however, not only forgot to restore their possessions to the unfortunate brothers, but began to oppress them in every way, and to extort from them all the treasures they had brought away from Kabul.

Amongst these the "Koh-i-Nûr" was coveted more than all the rest, and Runjît spared no efforts to get hold of it. How he at last effected his purpose is thus related by Kluge:—

"Driven from Peshawur to Kashmir, and hence to Lahore, Shah Shuja became apparently the guest, but in reality the prisoner of Runjit Singh, who, though no connoisseur of precious stones, none the less attached great importance to their possession. Of the 'Koh-i-Nûr' he had heard only by report, and employed every means to secure it. Woffo-Begum, consort of the unhappy king, had also sought and obtained protection from Runjit, and was consequently now residing in Shadera. Runjit ordered her to deliver up the stone, which, however, she protested was not in her possession. Thereupon he caused all her effects to be seized and brought to Lahore, thus acquiring jewels of greater value than any he had ever possessed before. Supposing that the 'Koh-i-Nûr' was amongst them, the bulk of the property, including shawls, carpets, and gems, was retained, and a few trifles returned to the Begum. But soon ascertaining that the 'Koh-i-Nûr' was not to be found amongst the jewels, he had the Begum closely watched; two of her most intimate attendants were thrown into prison, and the other members of the Zenana deprived even of bread and water. No one, without being first searched, was allowed to approach or leave the princess, and it was at the same time intimated, that nothing but the surrender of the diamond would satisfy Runjit. Thereupon the Begum sent him some very costly stones, and amongst them a ruby of considerable value. Having, as stated, no personal knowledge of gems, the tyrant of the Punjaub now fancied that this ruby, which surpassed everything he had yet seen, must be the real stone. But in order to make assurance doubly sure, he sent for a person acquainted with the Koh-i-Nûr, placed all the stones before him, and asked, which is the 'Koh-i-Nùr?' He received answer that it was not amongst those gems, which compared to it, were of little value. This made him all the more eager to procure it, and he again began to treat the Begum and her family with great harshness. After keeping them without food for two days, finding that she still held out, he gave up the hope of bringing her to terms by such means, and had recourse to more insinuating ways. She now promised to give up the stone, provided Runjît released Shah Shuja from captivity in Kashmir, and conferred a life pension on him, besides sundry favours on herself and friends. Shah Shuja was liberated at once, but some of the conditions not having been fulfilled, the Begum declared that the stone was not in her keeping, but that it had been pledged to a merchant in Kandahar. Runjît thereupon returned to the former coercive measures, and the princess was once more deprived of food, but all to no purpose. At last Shah Shuja himself volunteered to surrender the stone and a time was fixed, on which he promised to produce it.

"On June 1, 1813, the appointed day, Runjît, accompanied by several confidential friends, and some experts acquainted with the stone, proceeded to Shadera, where

Shah Shuja was then residing. At the en
suing interview, after both were seated, a
profound silence prevailed, which neither
side seemed disposed to break. An hour
was thus spent, and Runjît, notwithstanding his impatience, still abstained
from interrupting the solemn stillness.
He, however, hinted to a confidant that
he might quietly remind Shah Shuja
of the object of their interview. Thereupon the latter nodded to a slave, who
withdrew, and presently returning with
a packet, which he placed on the carpet,
at an equal distance from the two princes.
Deep silence again ensues; Runjît's impatience grows to a fever heat; no longer
able to control his feelings, he directs one
of the attendants to take up the packet;
it is opened, and a glittering gem of
unusual size is revealed, and recognised

by the experts as the true 'Koh-i-Nûr.'
At sight of the long-coveted prize, Runjît
forgets the past, and breaks the silence
with the question 'At what price do you
value it?' To which Shah Shuja replies
'At good luck, for it has ever been the
associate of him who has vanquished his
foes.' And he might have added with
equal truth, 'At bad luck, for sorrow and
sufferings have ever followed in its wake!'
But by his answer he betrayed the true
secret of the mysterious reverence akin to
worship, with which choice gems of this
sort have ever been regarded in the East,
and till recently in the West." Much in
the same way Marbœuf, bishop of Rennes,
in the 11th century, described in barbar-
ous Latin verse, the virtues of the Agate,
thus translated by King :—
"The Agate on the wearer strength bestows,
  With ruddy health his fresh complexion glows ;

The Koh-i-Nûr.

Both eloquence and grace by it are given,
He gains the favour both of earth and heaven."

According to the account of a trust-worthy eye-witness, Shah Shuja's bearing throughout this interview was such as to command the deepest respect, and pro-duced a marked effect upon the audience. He received from Runjît a sum of 125,000 rupees, and soon after this occurrence he withdrew with his brother, Shah Zâman, to Ludianah, in British territory, where they resided for some time on an annual pension of 60,000 rupees each, and 6,000 to each of their eldest sons. Here Whittaker tells us that he saw them in 1821, and he adds that Runjît at that time had the diamond at Lahore, capital of the Sikh States. " A Bengali shroff, or banker, named Sîlchûrd, resident at Ludianah, having occasion to visit Lahore on the Rajah's business, asked permission to see the jewel, which being granted, Sîlchûrd fell on his face and worshipped the stone."

The further adventures of this splendid gem are soon told. Runjît caused it to be set in a bracelet which he wore on all public occasions. On his death bed in 1839, an attempt was made to induce him to conciliate the favour of the gods by presenting the stone to the famous shrine of Jaganâth (Juggernaut). He is even said to have given his consent by an inclination of the head;* but the crown

---

* King (p. 73) puts another complexion on this story. According to him Runjît was so convinced that nothing but ruin would ever attend the possession of the fatal stone that, " having satisfied his covetousness in the enjoyment of its possession during his lifetime, he vainly sought to break through the ordinance of fate, and to avert the

34

jeweller refused to surrender the treasure
without a duly signed written warrant,
which was being prepared when Runjît
breathed his last. It thus remained in
the Lahore jewel-chamber till the young
Rajah Dhulîp-Singh was recognised by
the British Government(after the murder of
Shu-Singh),when an English Agent was sta-
tioned with a strong body-guard in Lahore.
Then followed the mutiny of the two Sikh
Regiments, which brought about the final
annexation of the Punjaub in 1849, when
as related by Hunt, "the civil authorities
took possession of the Lahore Treasury,

concomitant destruction from his family, by be-
queathing the stone to the shrine of Juggernaut
for the good of his soul and the preservation of
his dynasty. But his successors could not bring
themselves to give up the baleful treasure—each
one, doubtless, acting on the maxim 'après moi
le déluge.

under the stipulations previously made
that all the property of the State should
be confiscated to the East India Company, in part payment of the debt due
by the Lahore Government, and of the
expenses of the war. It was at the same
time stipulated that the 'Koh-i-Nûr' should
be presented to the Queen of England.
After the Company became possessed of
the gem, it was taken in charge by Lord
Dalhousie, and sent by him to England
in custody of two officers." Thus this
great historical diamond passed with
victory from East to West, and was presented to the future Kaiser-i-Hind on
June 3, 1850. It was shown at the first
great Exhibition held the following year
in Hyde Park, on which occasion it
attracted a great deal of attention,
although it had been so unskilfully treated

by the Indian cutter that it looked little better than an ordinary crystal.

When brought to Europe it was found to weigh exactly 186$\frac{1}{16}$ carats. We have seen that Baber gives the weight of Bikermâjit's diamond at "about eight mishkels," or somewhat over 187 carats, while Tavernier repeatedly declares that the "Great Mogul" was reduced by Borgio to 279 carats. Again the two stones were of totally different form, and the Mogul was without a history, having been quite recently discovered in the Kollur mine, whereas authentic records carried the "Koh-i-Nûr" back to the year 1304, beyond which date it had a tradition giving it an antiquity of some fifty centuries. Several recent writers still, however, persist in regarding these two distinct stones as one and the same gem. Even

Professor Nicol, in the last edition of the *Encyclopædia Britannica*, revives this theory, and goes the length of suggesting that the " Great Mogul," the " Koh-i-Nûr " and the stone found in Cûcha in 1832, were all pieces of one original crystal. Speaking of the " Koh-i-Nûr," he remarks that "its lower side is flat and undoubtedly corresponds to a cleavage plane. Hence it has been conjectured that it and the Russian " Orloff" diamond are portions of the original stone belonging to the 'Great Mogul,' whilst a stone of 132 carats obtained by Abbas Mirza at the storming of Cûcha in Khorassan in 1832, may be a third fragment. This portion was long used by a peasant as a flint for striking fire. The three united would have nearly the form and size given by Tavernier, and the ' Koh-i-Nûr' would then surpass all known diamonds in its magnitude, as in its eventful history." For a refutation of this theory, the reader is referred to our account of the Abbas Mîrza Diamond.

In consequence of the clumsy way in which the Hindoo cutter had handled the "Koh-i-Nûr," at a time when the art was still, doubtless, in its infancy, Prince Albert consulted Sir David Brewster, as to how it might be re-cut to the best possible advantage. He found in it, as is the case with many other large diamonds, several little cavities, which he declared (according to his theory), to be the result of the expansive force of con-densed gases. This, together with the flaws already noticed, he considered would make the cutting of it, without serious diminution, a very difficult thing. Messrs. Coster, however, of Amsterdam, thought that in the hands of skilful workmen, the difficulties might be overcome. Several patterns were laid before Her Majesty and the Prince Consort, and after due consultation, selection was made of the form which it now has, and which may be described as that of a regularly cut brilliant.

Mr. Voorsanger, of Coster's establishment, was the workman entrusted with the responsible task of re-cutting this famous gem, and his labours were conducted in the *atelier* of one of the jewellers in London. To assist his object a small four-horse machine was erected, and the cutting commenced by the Prince Consort placing the diamond on the mill on the 6th of July, 1852. The operation was completed at the end of thirty-eight days of twelve hours each. The "Star of the

South," a much larger stone, was afterwards cut by Messrs. Coster in three
months. The "Pitt," or "Regent,'
treated by the slower hand-process of the
eighteenth century, had occupied no less
than two years.

One of the flaws in the "Koh-i-Nûr"
gave great trouble. In order to remove it
the number of revolutions of the cutting-
wheel had to be increased to 3,000 per
minute, and even then the object was only
attained very slowly. During the process
of reduction, the diamond lost exactly
eighty carats in weight, having been reduced from 186$\frac{1}{16}$ carats to its present
weight of 106$\frac{1}{16}$ carats.

After all, the result was far from giving
universal satisfaction, although obtained
at a cost of no less than £8,000. The
Prince Consort, who took the greatest

interest in the operation, and whose sound advice had probably prevented a total failure, openly expressed his dissatisfaction with the work.

On the treatment which the "Koh-i-Nûr" received in the cutter's hands, the late Mr. King is very severe, remarking that owing to the flattened and oval figure of the stone, the brilliant pattern selected by the Queen's advisers "entailed the greatest possible amount of waste." He adds that Mr. Coster would have preferred the drop form, but that "in a historical relic like this, the sole course that would have recommended itself to a person of taste, was the judicious one pursued some years before by Messrs. Rundell and Bridge, in their re-cutting of the "Nassak," both in its native and artificial figure. In this, by following the trails of the Hindoo cutter, amending his defects, and accommodating the pattern to the exigencies of the subject matter, they transformed the rudely-facetted, lustreless mass, into a diamond of perfect brilliancy, at the sacrifice of no more than ten per cent of its original weight."

It may also be remarked that, although said to be cut as a brilliant, this great Oriental talisman is really only such in name, being much too thin to have satisfied the Jeffries, Ralph Potters, and the other great dealers of the last and beginning of the present century. In fact the cutting of the "Koh-i-Nûr" on this occasion, revealed the painful fact that the art was then extinct in England, while even the Amsterdam and Paris operators had lost much of their former cunning. They followed a system of mere routine, betraying

43

little inventive power, and showing themselves incapable of grappling with the problem of how best to reduce a stone, with the least sacrifice of its weight, and the greatest display of its natural lustre.

The " Koh-i-Nûr " is preserved in Windsor Castle. A model of the gem is kept in the jewel room of the Tower of London, to satisfy the laudable curiosity of Her Majesty's faithful lieges. Although not of the very finest water, and of a greyish tinge, the stone was valued before being re-cut at about £140,000. But Barbot considers it far from being worth such a sum. He allows, however, that it is still an extraordinary stone, "but more on account of its great surface than for its play, which is almost neutralised by its great spread." It must, however, be remembered that this is the criticism of a

44

The Koh-i-Nûr.

Frenchman naturally alarmed for the hitherto unrivalled reputation of the "Regent" or "Pitt." Since Barbot's time it will be seen in our account of the "English Dresden," that the lustre even of the "Regent," has been somewhat dimmed by the absolutely faultless character of the Bagagem crystal.

Although yielding to these and perhaps to one or two others in brilliancy, as it does to several in size, the "Koh-i-Nûr" must ever remain without a rival for the intense interest attaching to the sanguinary and romantic incidents associated with its marvellous career. A strange fatality presided over its early vicissitudes, but its alleged "uncannie" powers have now ceased to be a subject of apprehension. Its latest history eloquently demonstrates the fact that extended empire is a blessing,

45

just in proportion as it finds hearts and hands willing to fulfil the high duties which increased privileges involve.

The Koh-i-Nûr.

GEOLOGICAL MUSEUM,
Trinity College, Dublin.
13th September, 1882.

Dear Sir,

The copy of your book which you so kindly sent me reached me quite safely at Southampton. I have read it very carefully and have detected a few misprints, and there are some points upon which I should like to make some remarks. I am sorry that in quoting from me you did not do so from my books or the papers I sent you. One of my identifications mentioned in my letter to *Nature,* namely Raolconda, I found subsequently was incorrect. It is not the modern Rawdakonda, but Ramulkta, a spot in Karnul, where there have been extensive mines. Last week's *Nature* gave a wholly incorrect account of a paper I read at the British Association, it was from an uncorrected proof abstract containing several errors. What I said about the Great Mogul and Koh-i-Nûr question was by no means so emphatic. I am inclined to think that your case against their identity is almost conclusive. At any rate it makes proof of the identity impossible.

Your whole work, if you will allow me to say so, is an enormous improvement on any that has been written.

Yours faithfully,

(*Signed*), J. Ball.

The Koh-i-Nûr.

SCIENCE & ART MUSEUM, Dublin,
18th November, 1886.
Dear Sir,

In your work on the Great Diamonds on p. 33, 1st Ed. The source of the story about diamonds having been found in Malacca is said to have originated in an incidental reference to Malachite. The story is traceable as far back as De Boot, 1609, and beyond it I have not been able to travel. Would you kindly aid me by letting me know to whom the Malachite jumble has been traced.

A friend in Malacca has been trying to aid me but without success. I asked him in consequence of Miss Bird (Golden Chersonese) saying that diamonds are occasionally found in Malacca

Since I was in correspondence with you some years ago, I have made a large number of additional identifications with reference to Indian Diamonds, &c.

Yours faithfully,
(*Signed*)　J. BALL.

XVIII

THE PITT:

Its History and Romance.

First known as the "Pitt," then as the "Regent," this perfect diamond has a remarkable history. There are two stories of its original discovery. They do not differ sufficiently to cast a doubt upon the general facts. The second version of the narrative is easily reconcilable with the first

The adventures of the "Pitt" begin very much on the lines of several other great stones. Cupidity, murder, remorse, are factors in the opening chapter. Trouble, political, social, and personal, accompany the gem to its latest resting-place. It was found by a slave in the Parteal mines, on the Kistna, in the year 1701. The story goes that, to secure his treasure, he cut a hole in the calf of his leg, and concealed it, one account says, in the wound itself, another in the bandages.

As the stone weighed 410 carats before it was cut, the last version of the method of concealment is, no doubt, the correct one. The slave escaped to the coast with his property. Unfortunately for himself and also for the peace of mind of his confidant, he met with an English skipper, whom he trusted with his secret. It is said he offered to give the diamond to the mariner, in return for his liberty, which was to be secured by the skipper carrying him to a free country. But it seems probable that he supplemented this with a money condition as well, otherwise the skipper's treatment of the poor creature is as devoid of reason as it is of humanity· The English skipper, professing to accept the slave's proposals, took him on board his ship, and having obtained possession of the jewel, flung the slave into the sea.

He afterwards, so this first version of the narrative goes, sold the diamond to Mr. Thomas Pitt, governor of Fort St. George, for £1,000, squandered the money in dissipation, and finally, in a fit of *delirium tremens* and remorse, hanged himself.

There is no reason to doubt the substantial accuracy of this characteristic beginning of the adventures of the great diamond, with a trifling exception. The English sea captain sold it in all probability for £1,000, not to Mr. Pitt, but to Jamchund, at that time the largest diamond merchant in the East, who, it will be seen in the course of our history, sold it to Mr. Pitt for £20,400. The circumstances connected with his purchase of the gem, are fully related by Pitt himself, who, on his return to Europe in 1710, was suspected, and even openly accused, of having procured it by foul or unfair means. Amongst others Pope was supposed to point at something of the kind in the oft-quoted lines from the *Man of Ross.*

"Asleep and naked as an Indian lay,
An honest factor stole a gem away;
He pledg'd it to the Knight, the Knight had wit,
So kept the diamond, and the rogue was bit."

These scandalous reports, to which however much credence never seems to have been attached, having reached the ex-governor, at that time in Norway, he sent a letter from Bergen to the editor of the *European Magazine* for October, 1710, setting forth the true facts of the case. A certified copy of this document was carefully preserved in the Pitt family, and, in consequence of some fresh rumours regarding the early history of the diamond, was again published by them in the *Daily Post* for November 3, 1743, that is, seventeen years after Pitt's death. The chief passages bearing on the transaction are here subjoined from the latter source :—

"Since my coming into this melancholy place of Bergen, I have been often thinking of the most unparalleled villainy of William Fraser, Thomas Frederick, and Sampa, a black merchant, who brought a paper before Governor Addison* in council, insinuating that I had unfairly got possession of a large diamond, which tended so much to the prejudice of my reputation, and the ruin of my estate, that I thought necesary to keep by me the true relation how I purchased it in all respects, that so in case of sudden mortality, my

---

* This was a brother of the celebrated poet and essayist. He succeeded Pitt as governor of Fort St. George in 1709 or 1710.

children and friends may be apprized of the whole matter, and so be enabled thereby to put to silence and confound those and all other villains, in their base attempts against either.

"About two or three years after my arrival at Madras, which was in July, 1698, I heard there were large diamonds in the country to be sold, which I encouraged to be brought down, promising to be their chaperon, if they would be reasonable therein, upon which Jamchund, one of the most eminent diamond merchants in these parts, came down about December, 1701, and brought with him a large rough stone, about 305 mangelins, and some small ones, which myself and others bought. But he asking a very extravagant price for the great one, I did not think of meddling with it; when he left it with me for some days, and then came and took it away again, and did so several times, insisting upon not less than 200,000 pagodas,* and as I best remember, I did not bid him more than 30,000, and had little thoughts of buying it for that. I considered there were many and great risks to be run, not only in cutting it, but whether it would prove foul or clean, or the water good. Besides, I thought it too great an amount to venture home in one bottom, so that Jamchund resolved to return speedily to his own country, so that, I best remember, it was in February following he came again to me (with Vincaty Chittee, who was always with him when I discoursed about it), and pressed me to know whether I resolved to buy it,

---

* As a pagoda is worth about 8s. 6d., this would be equivalent to about £85,000

when he came down to 100,000 padagoes,
and something under before we parted,
when we agreed upon a day to meet and
to make a final end thereof, one way or
other, which I believe was the latter end
of the aforesaid month, or beginning of
March, when we met in the consultation
room, when, after a great deal of talk, I
brought him down to 55,000 padagoes,
and advanced to 45,000, resolving to give
no more and he likewise not to abate, so
delivered him up the stone, and we took a
friendly leave of one another   Mr. Benyon
was then writing in my closet, with whom
I discoursed what had passed, and told
him now I was clear of it ; when, about
half-an-hour after, my servant brought
me word that Jamchund and Vincaty
Chittee were at the door, who, being
called in, they used a great many

expressions in praise of the stone, and told me he had rather I should buy it than anybody ; and, to give an instance thereof, offered it for 50,000. So, believing it must be a pennyworth if it proved good, I offered to part the 5,000 padagoes that were between us, which he would not hearken to, and was going out of the room again, when he turned back, and told me I should have it for 49,000. But I still adhered to what I had before offered him, when presently he came to 48,000, and made a solemn vow he would not part with it for a padagoe under ; when I went again into the closet to Mr. Benyon, and told him what had passed, saying that if it was worth 47,500 it was worth 48,000.*

---

* Pitt, who throughout spells "padagoe" for pagoda, here appends a note in which he reduces the 48,000 pagodas to " £20,400 sterling, at 8s. 6d. per padagoe."

So I closed with him for that sum, when he delivered me the stone, for which I paid him honourably, as by my books doth appear. And I here further call God to witness that I never used the least threatening word at any of our meetings to induce him to sell it to me; and God Himself knows it was never so much as in my thoughts so to do. Since which I have had frequent and considerable dealings with this man, and trusted him with several sums of money, and balanced several accounts with him, and left upwards of 2,000 padagoes in his hands at my coming away. So had I used the least indirect means to have got it from him, would he not have made himself satisfaction, when he has had my money so often in his hands? Or would I have trusted him afterwards, as I did preferable to all other diamond merchants? As this is the truth, so I hope for God's blessing upon this and all my other affairs in this world, and eternal happiness hereafter.—Written and signed by me in Bergen, July 29, 1710.— THO. PITT."

On the back of this declaration the following words are written:—"In case of the death of me, Tho. Pitt, I direct that this paper, sealed as it is, be delivered to my son, Robert Pitt.

In publishing this document the editor of the *Daily Post* observes that he does so "at this time of day" (that is seventeen years after Pitt's death), "by desire, and hopes that the following piece will give satisfaction to all those who may still suspect that that gentleman did not fairly come by the said stone.

No doubt Pitt drove rather a hard

bargain with Jamchund; but there was otherwise nothing dishonourable or even unusual in the transaction. It will be noticed that in this account there is no reference to the story of the slave, about which neither Pitt nor Jamchund were likely to know anything. The governor was evidently under the impression that the dealer had brought the stone with many others down from the diamond-fields, while the dealer, if he picked up such a gem for £1,000 from a sea captain on the coast, would naturally abstain from asking any indiscreet questions, whatever his suspicions might be. The fact that Jamchund ultimately closed for 48,000 pagodas, or a little over £20,000, after asking 200,000, pagodas, or £85,000, would almost imply that he was glad to get rid of the diamond "at a sacrifice," because conscious that the circumstances attending its purchase would not bear any severe scrutiny.

Pitt's account of his share in the transaction was afterwards fully confirmed by Mr. Salmon who was present on the occasion. Yet it appears that the stone which had been consigned by Pitt to Sir Stephen Evance, of London, and sent home in the ship *Bedford*, (Captain John Hudson), was charged in the original bill of lading at 6,500 pagodas only. This might have been done either to save freight, or more probably to avoid attracting attention to the stone, and thereby exposing it to the risk of being stolen.

The diamond was cut very skilfully in London, and in the process, which lasted two years, it was reduced from 410 to $136\frac{3}{4}$ carats. The editor of the *Museum*

Britannicum stated at the time that the cutting and polishing cost £5,000, and Jeffries, who points out the mistake made in the operation, and shows how it might be improved, remarks that there is only one small speck, and that placed in such a position as not to be detected in the setting. He says also that another £5,000 was spent in negotiating its sale to the Regent, Duke of Orleans, who purchased it in 1717, during the minority of Louis XV., for £135,000. The cleavage and dust obtained in the cutting were also valued at from £7,000 to £8,000,* so

---

* These figures, like almost everything else connected with the history of the great historical diamonds, are variously given in different writers. Thus Murray (p. 59) gives, as here stated, "from £7,000 to £8,000;" while King (p. 83) says that "the value of the fragments separated in shaping it, amounted to £3,500." He adds that it became

that Pitt must have netted at least
£100,000 by his venture. With this he
restored the fortunes of the ancient house
of Pitt, which was destined later on to
give to England two of her greatest states-
men and orators, for the governor of Fort
St. George was grandfather of the great
Earl of Chatham, father of the illustrious
William Pitt. He was born at Blandford,
in Dorsetshire, where he was buried in
May, 1726. In the funeral oration
preached on the occasion by the Rev.
Canon R. Eyre, the following reference
was made to the "diamond scandal:"—
"That he should have enemies no wonder,
when envy will make them, and when
their malice could reach him in no other

by the process, "for perfection of shape as well
as for purity of water the first diamond in the
world ; as it still continues.'

way, it is as little to be wondered at that they should make such an attempt upon his credit by an abusive story as if it had been by some stretch of his power that he got that diamond which was of too great a value for any subject to purchase, an ornament more fitly becoming an Imperial crown, which if it be considered, may be one reason why it was brought to the governor by the merchant who sold it in the Indies, and it was brought to him once or twice before he could be persuaded to part with so great a sum of money for it, as it cost him."

Even after refuting the calumnies of his enemies, Pitt knew little rest until he was quit of his costly jewel. He was constantly haunted by a morbid fear of losing or being robbed of it so that it was with great difficulty he could ever be

66

induced to exhibit it even to his most intimate friends. The German traveller, Offenbach, when visiting England in 1712, anxious to see all the sights of the metropolis, made several vain attempts to get a view of the gem, which had already become famous throughout the West. While it remained in his possession the ex-governor never slept two nights running under the same roof. He moved about capriciously, or in disguise, and never gave previous notice of his arrival to, or departure from town.

At last he was relieved of further anxiety by the negotiations, in consequence of which the " Pitt " became, the "Regent," passing from its English owner into the hands of the Duke of Orleans, Regent of France, in 1717. After being cut in the form of an almost faultless brilliant, a

model of the diamond was taken, which
is now in the British Museum,* and on
the silver frame is engraved the legend:
" This is the model of Governor Pitt's
diamond, weight 136½ carats; was sold to
Louis XV. of France, A.D. 1717." This
model, or rather a duplicate without the
frame, had been sent to Paris and submitted to the famous Scotch financier
John Law, at that time at the height
of his power in France. Law took the
stone first to the Regent, and then to the
Duc de Saint Simon,† who gives a full

---

* Murray (p. 65) says that in the same place
there is another " model of the 'Pitt' in its original
rough form in lead."

† Saint Simon, who seems to have known
nothing of its early history, asserts that it was
stolen by a person employed in the Indian
diamond fields, who brought it to Europe. After

account of the affair in his *Memoirs*. Saint Simon agreed with Law that France ought to possess a gem which up to that time was incomparably the finest ever seen in Europe. Yielding to their combined efforts, the Regent at last consented to purchase it for £135,000,* including £5,000 for the negotiations, a euphemistic expression, which, translated into plain language, meant a bribe for Law. Money, however, was just then so scarce, that the

---

showing it to the King of England, and several other English noblemen, he took it to Paris, where he submitted it to Law. Then follow the particulars of the negotiations with the French Regent, as stated in the text.

* But on this point the authorities are at variance with each other. Board says the figure was 2,250,000 francs; Jeffries £125,000; others £130,000.

interest alone was paid on the amount, jewels being given as security for the principal until it was paid off. This price, great as it may appear to be, was even then regarded as much below its real value, and in the inventory of the French Crown Jewels, drawn up in 1791, it is valued at 12,000,000 francs, or £480,000.

The year after the preparation of this inventory which was made by a commission of the most experienced jewellers in Paris, the whole of the French Regalia disappeared, and with it the " Pitt," now the " Regent," which stood at the head of the list. The remarkable circumstances attending this famous robbery of the *Garde-Meuble* are thus related by M. Breton, editor of the *Gazette des Tribuneaux* :—

" The inventory of the Crown diamonds, made in 1791, in virtue of a degree of the Constituent Assembly, had scarcely been completed in the month of August, 1792, at the time of the last public exhibition, which took place on the first Tuesday of every month. After the sanguinary events of August 10th to September 2nd, this rich treasury was naturally closed to the public, and the Paris Commune, as representing the State property, put its seals on the cabinets in which had been placed the crown, the sceptre, and other ornaments of the coronation service. The golden shrine, bequeathed by Cardinal Richelieu to Louis XIII., with all the accompanying diamonds and rubies, and the famous golden vase, weighing 106 marks, besides a vast quantity of other vases in agate, amethyst, and rock crystal. On the morning of September 17th, Sergent and the two other commissioners of the

Commune, perceived that during the night robbers had made their way in by scaling the colonnade from the side of the Place Louis XV., and through a window looking in that direction. Having thus got access to the vast halls of the Garde-Meuble, they had broken the seals without forcing the locks, carried off the priceless treasures contained in the cabinets, and disappeared without leaving any other traces of their presence. Several persons were arrested, but released after a protracted enquiry. An anonymous letter, addressed to the Commune stated, that some of the stolen objects were in a ditch in the Allée des Veuves, Champs-Elysées. Sergent at once proceeded with his colleagues to the spot, which had been very carefully indicated. Here were found amongst other thing the famous " Regent " diamond, and the no less famous agate onyx cup, known by the name of the Abbé Suger's Chalice, which was afterwards placed in the cabinet of antiques in the National Library.

"Notwithstanding the investigations made at the time and subsequently, it remained uncertain whether this robbery had a political object, or whether it was simply the act of ordinary criminals, undertaken at a time when the guardians of the public security were in a state of complete disorganization. Some said that the proceeds of these treasures were intended to maintain the army of the emigrants. Others, on the contrary, pretended that Pethion and Manual had used them to obtain the evacuation of Champagne, by giving up the whole to the King of Prussia. Some even went so far as to assert that the keepers themselves had broken open the cabinets, and Sergent. of whom we have above spoken, was nick-named *Agate*, in consequence of the mysterious way in which he had found the agate-onyx cup. But none of these more or less absurd surmises ever received any judicial confirmation."

"Nevertheless, there was one circumstance of which I was witness, jointly with the others present at the sitting of the special criminal court of Paris, when Bourgeoise and others accused of having forged notes on the Bank of France, were put upon their trial in 1804. One of the accused, who had assumed the name of *Baba*, had at first denied all the charges brought against him. But during the proceedings he made a complete confession and explained the ingenious devices employed by the forgers. ' It is not the first

time,' he added, ' that my revelations have
been useful to society, and if I am now
condemned, I will implore the emperor's
pardon. But for me, Napoleon would
never have mounted the throne; to me
alone is due the success of the Marengo
campaign. I was one of the robbers of
the Garde-Meuble. I had assisted my
associates to bury in the Allé des Veuves the
' Regent ' and the other easily recognized
objects, by which they might have been
betrayed. On the promise of a free pardon,
a promise which was faithfully kept, I
disclosed the hiding-place. Here the
' Regent ' was recovered, and you are
aware, gentlemen, that this magnificent
diamond was pledged by the first Consul
to the Dutch Government, in order to
raise the money, of which he stood in the
greatest need after the 18th Brumaire."

"'The criminals were all condemned to the galleys except Bourgeois and Baba, who were sent to the prison of Bicêtre, where they died. I do not know whether Baba made any further revelations beyond what I have reported, and which may also be read in the *Journal de Paris* of that date."

Since its recovery and redemption from the Dutch Government, the "Regent" seems to have remained in the French treasury to the present time. The first emperor is known to have worn it in the pommel of his sword, and Barbot tells us expressly that it was publicly shown amongst the Crown jewellery, at the Paris Exhibition of 1855.* Still it is remarkable

---

* "Tout le monde a pu admirer cette magnifique pierre parmi les parures de la couronne à

that this brilliant does not figure in the inventory of the State Jewels, drawn up by order of Napoleon in 1810, nor apparently in any of the subsequent official reports on the Crown jewels. This circumstance, however it is to be explained, has doubtless, lent some colouring to the many conflicting statements regarding its subsequent vicissitudes. Kluge asserts that

---

sa rare et unique beauté." Op. cit. p. 240. Touching its "rare and singular beauty." this writer, a most competent judge in such matters, adds (p.44), "ce qui fait la valeur du 'Regent' ne gît pas seulement dans son poids mais bien en ce qu'il est l'unique parmi toutes les pierres princièpes, réunissant les plus rares qualitiés des gros diamants, c'est-à-dire blancheur éclat et surtout beauté de forme. Il en est certes plus volumineux, l'Exposition Universelle de 1855, et contempler mais s'il fallait les ramener à la pureté de forme du 'Regent' aucun n'atteindrait son poids."

after its recovery in 1792, it was pledged, not to the Dutch Government, but to Treskow, a merchant in Berlin. He also refers to the highly improbable report that, after the battle of Waterloo, where the Prussians found it in the Emperor's State carriage, it was carried off to the Prussian treasury. If it really was taken to Berlin on that occasion, it was subsequently restored to the French Government for Ersch and Gruber, writing in 1833, distinctly state that at that time it was "the first diamond in the French treasury."* Barbot also justly regards it as the most conspicuous gem in the now disused crown of France. This crown, which also contains eight other diamonds,

---

* "Er ist der erste Diamant im französischen Schatze." *Allegemeine Encyclopädie.* Vol. 24, p. 456.

weighing from 19 to 28 carats, is thus by far the richest in the world.*

The form of the " Regent," is somewhat round, an inch broad, $1\frac{1}{6}$ of an inch long, and $\frac{3}{4}$ of an inch thick. It was reduced in cutting from 410 to $136\frac{1}{8}$ carats, and has been estimated to be worth £480,000.

---

* The Ministry of Finance was visited this afternoon by the Parliamentary Committee entrusted with the examination of the bill relative to the sale of the Crown Jewels. The committee was received by M. Antonin Proust and by MM. Bapst, the jewellers, who gave it all the necessary information. It appears that during the Restoration the Crown jewels were deposited with the Bapst. Under Louis Philippe they were kept in the Garde Meuble, and during the Empire, M. Thélin had them safely locked up in a strong box. They are now in chests in a cellar at the Ministry of Finance, and it is in this subterranean chamber that they were laid out to-day. The ornaments that possess a historic or an artistic value had

been separated from the rest. They include a collection of decorations sent to the sovereigns of France by foreign monarchs, and are valued at £8,000 sterling ; a watch presented by the Dey of Algiers to Louis Quatorze and worth £120; a brooch of diamonds, of antique cut, valued at about £3,000 ; and a sword, the hilt of which, mounted in 1824, is a fine specimen of chaste French workmanship. MM. Bapst advised the committee to retain all these articles, as they were really worth far more than their money value. There is, consequently, every reason to believe that they will eventually find their way to the Apollo Gallery at the Louvre. As for the "Regent," a diamond unique in the world on account of its size, the jewellers also opposed its sale. It was formerly valued as high as half a million sterling, but there is always risk that it might not fetch more than £25,000, and its acquisition by some enterprising showman would be scarcely creditable to this country. Such were the arguments used by MM Bapst, and their counsels will probably be followed in this as in other matters. The other jewels, estimated—*en bloc*—at about half a million pounds, have no historic value. There are only three parures, the sapphire, the turquoise, and the ruby parure, the last made expressly for the Duchesse de Berry. All the other jewels were arranged and altered again and again, to suit the taste of the Empress Eugénie. I may add that the committee has not yet arrived at any definite decision, but will revisit the Crown jewels in the course of the week.—"Paris Correspondent," *Daily Telegraph,* *December* 8, 1881.

It was decided by the Republic not to sell the Pitt diamond, and it is now to be seen at the Louvre in Paris.

PRECIOUS STONES AND GEMS.

Reviews.

THE STANDARD.—" Mr. Streeter gives an accurate and complete description of every kind of Precious Stone and Gem known, and makes his book still more attractive and complete by a series of coloured plates of several stones in the rough."

THE DAILY TELEGRAPH.—"Considers the knowledge and experience of Mr. Streeter usefully displayed for the information of all.

THE DAILY NEWS.—" Few romances, indeed, can be more entertaining, though the primary object of the volume is strictly of a practical kind."

THE MORNING POST.—" Mr. Streeter prefaces his handsome volume with a warning to his readers that it is not intended as a scientific treatise, but a practical work on the nature, properties, and value of Precious Stones."

THE MORNING ADVERTISER.—" This Volume may be taken for the future as the text book of lapidarian lore."

Opinions of the Press.

THE ST. JAMES'S GAZETTE.—"There are several chapters in Mr. Streeter's book on South African, Australian, Brazilian, and Indian Diamonds; and as many more on coloured, the geological as well as the geographical regions in which they are found being clearly stated."

THE SATURDAY REVIEW.—"The valuable part of Mr. Streeter's book is that which relates to the diamond-producing countries.'

THE GRAPHIC.—"As a manual of gems; their market price and characteristics. . . . . Mr. Streeter's book claims a speciality among the crowd of books about Precious Stones."

THE OBSERVER. — "Mr. Streeter is to be congratulated upon having made his history and characteristics of gems exceedingly interesting, but also for having provided a manual of the greatest possible use."

THE QUEEN.—"The plan of this new book is so comprehensive that it includes very full details on many topics. The notes on coloured diamonds are very interesting."

PEARLS AND PEARLING LIFE.

Reviews.

THE WORLD.—"Mr. Streeter is the author of 'Pearls and Pearling Life,' gives much curious information as to the pearling-grounds, the diving, and the treatment of the pearl." Dec. 13th, 1886.

THE COURT JOURNAL.—This work tests that Mr. Streeter has the spirit of the explorer." Dec. 18th, 1886.

THE SUNDAY TIMES.—"Mr. Streeter has gone deep into the subject. The illustrations have a recognizable value especially that of the pearl known as the Southern Cross." Dec. 19th, 1886.

THE DAILY TELEGRAPH.—"The account of the pearl fishing, is interesting, As a practical man Mr. Streeter thoroughly understands his subject. Dec. 28th, 1886.

THE MORNING POST.—"Pearls and Pearling Life is interesting to such of the public as may wish to acquire a knowledge of the history and formation of the pearl. Dec. 25th, 1886.

Opinions of the Press.

VANITY FAIR.—" Mr. Streeter writes as a practical man and gives us facts and criticisms at first hand." Dec. 25th, 1886.

THE PICTORIAL WORLD.—" Mr. Streeter has a fleet engaged in pearl fishing in Sooloo Archipelago, off the coast of N.W. Australia." Dec. 30th, 1886.

THE ST. JAMES'S GAZETTE.—" With regard to Pearling Life the author gives an exhaustive account of the fisheries." Dec. 3rd, 1886.

THE GRAPHIC.—" Mr. Streeter in Pearls and Pearling Life deals with the vexed question of their formation. Jan. 29th, 1887'

THE QUEEN.—" The author who has a fleet of vessels engaged in the trade has had exceptional opportunities for acquiring information, and some of his facts are altogether remarkable. March 5th, 1887.

THE DAILY NEWS.—" In 'Pearls and Pearling Life' Mr. Streeter gives an interesting account of Pearls, their homes, their qualities, their beauties and their origin, and the manner of fishing for them." March 11th, 1887.

www.ingramcontent.com/pod-product-compliance
Lightning Source LLC
Chambersburg PA
CBHW020327090426
42735CB00009B/1434